Becoming a Manager of My Time

BENITA SMITH

DEDICATION

TO MY DAUGHTERS AND GRANDDAUGHTER –
LOVE YOU SO MUCH!
I AM INTENTIONALLY CREATING MOMENTS WE
WILL REMEMBER FOREVER.

*Create intentional
memories every day*

****

About the Author – Benita Smith

- Email: coachbenitas@gmail.com
- Instagram: @CoachBenitaS
- Life Coach specializing in transforming Communication between Mothers & Daughters

Time Management is a personal subject for me. It is essential that I share this simple and easy process with you, so that you can live your life now. Many people feel they must wait for a milestone to begin to live. Have you heard "When I retire, I will start to travel the world". If you are reading this right now, you can begin to live today. My purpose is to make sure you are creating great memories for those around you because memories last forever.

Congratulations and welcome to becoming a Manager of Your Time.

You are embarking on a wonderful journey with me and I hope that you are ready to tackle some areas in your life that need a few adjustments and some fine tuning. Use this guide as motivation to achieve your goals and dreams.

We are all managers of our time. The concept of managing all your time can be an impossible feat and can be overwhelming to many people. Your days can blend and create a sense of feeling like you have not accomplished much during you day. Here are a couple questions that I want you to ponder:

- Do you have free time to be adventurous?
- What if someone calls you with an emergency, can you truly be there for that person?

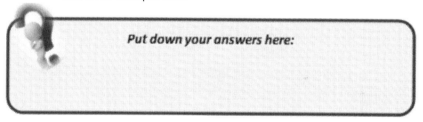

Put down your answers here:

Typical responses when you ask people if they have time:

- *"I don't have any time"*
- *"I wish there was more hours in the day"*
- *"Time got away from me"*

Have you used some of these responses when answering others? Well, today you can throw away these responses after you become a manager of your time.

> *Many people say that "Time got away from me?"*
>
> *What are some of your responses when someone asks you about your time?*

How to begin: We will start first with defining the word management. When I use the word management, I usually think of someone in charge of a process. The manager would create the vision and control the process. When it comes to the vision, the manager must keep the "end" result in mind. When it comes to changes and enhancements, the manager must execute those steps.

Reflection: Right now –close your eyes and think back to a time when you were in a happy and content place. Staying in that moment think about who was present, how you felt, how long did it last and would you like to have that moment again. If you could repeat that moment, would you change anything? Would you want a different ending to the moment? Let me share a personal story that is truly MY WHY of being a manager of my time. My first effort of being a great manager of my time occurred during my freshman year of college. Beginning college was a new beginning of a life cycle for me and I truly embraced it with true happiness. I was very excited about the many aspects of the "college lifestyle": academics, social and athletics. Life could not have been more perfect! Well there was a huge issue that I had to overcome and did not know where to start. I struggled with my study time, social time and athletic time. All three were equally important to me. I could not choose from one item to the next. Prioritizing them was not an option since all of them filled up my days. I had to study to be successful in my freshman courses and make sure I would pass the quizzes and tests. I knew being socially active with my roommates and being involved on campus would help me not feel home sick. And lastly, I knew that I wanted to be on top of my game when it came to my athletic efforts, so I had to be more mindful of my time and get results needed to progress forward in the rankings. The point I am making here is that all three of these items felt impossible to manage and so I turned to my coach at the time to help me with this struggle. He suggested a time management class which at the time used the Franklin planner.

This is a paper method of planning your day and it literally made me a terrific manager of my time. I was able to accomplish all three priorities using the effective time management processes and being fully present in the moments that matter most to me during my college life. Over the years and as life has changed, I have incorporated my own spin to the time management process and have helped many people understand the concepts and practical use of the steps.

3 Objectives you will learn:

- Write down your short, mid and long-term goals that you want to achieve. Also include a financial goal as well. The time you track should show how you are accomplishing these goals. If you find that your weekly table does not align with your goals, then you should re-think what you do every week. We do not get this time back, so make the best out of it. Achieve your goals and manage your time properly.
- Make room for your dreams. Dare to dream and see how you can find time to achieve these

This may come as a surprise to some but not to all. Depending on how you think about your time and how it is managed, the process can be very overwhelming. So, consider this acronym when thinking about becoming a manager of your time:

TIME

Take In Moments

Everyday

Goals:

Short Term, Mid and Long-Term (include financial goal)

Warning signs when time management is needed:

- You set goals and/or have dreams and have not accomplished them and every year seems to be the same story. Let's get rid of all the excuses.
- You find yourself spending time with others and you are not fully present. You are either on the phone or daydreaming.
- You find that when you give someone your word that you will spend time with them, you find yourself regretting the decision in the midst of the visit and it seems to be a repeated action on your part. You may be losing friendships because of this action.

Whenever I think about becoming a manager of my time, my thoughts go back to knowing how precious time is in a single day. My hope is that this process will be a helpful guide to your journey to become aware of how you spend your time.

You are probably interested in this topic because someone may have asked you for more time or you are tired of seeing your days go by without feeling like you have accomplished nothing. Believe it or not, you are spending time accomplishing things in every moment, it just may not be the thing you want to accomplish.

We will work with a total of 4 tables in 3 phases. It is important to follow the steps in order to fully understand the process of time management.

PHASE ONE: Pre-Work

Let's dive right in! We will start with Table One which is referred as "Pre-Work". Your Pre-Work will represent a typical week. It's important to track a typical week that you will experience to ensure next steps through this process. Make sure you complete this Pre-Work to the best of your ability and to follow the steps below precisely. If done accurately, it will help you to see the time spent on activities and help you decide where the changes can take place. Follow the instructions below and do not change categorized items for the sake of reviewing results and data analytics which we will discuss later. Believe me, you will love this concept and appreciate the set categories.

Instructions for TABLE ONE: PRE-WORK:

STEP ONE: Fill out "Table One: Pre-Work" (page 13)
Use these categorized items (**Work, Activity, Transit, Lunch, Sleep, Home**) to track your normal schedule for the week. Remember do not change categorized items for the purposes of tracking and reviewing. We will track our time hourly for this exercise. You can use highlighters to show your different categories.

a) **Work** = Make sure to account for hours you work in the table. If you do not work, use this category to account for time spent outside of the house. If you work from home, record your hours worked. This represents time spent on an activity that is something you do every week almost at the same time (ex: volunteering, book club, coffee shop, errands)

Although tracking is based hourly, try to use your imagination to account for your "regular" daily activity each hour. Of course, your travel time to work may not take an entire hour but putting it down for one hour would still work for this exercise.

b) **Activity** = Input all activities that you are required to attend. List any paid for activities (ex: gym, music class, children's/partner's activities). This activity cannot be moved, or you prefer it not to be moved. This does not include time with family, friends, etc. If we are honest, spending time with others can be changed.

c) **Transit** = Put this in your chart as your means to travel to work, activity and home.

d) **Lunch** = Please take a lunch every day. If you take ½ hour lunch then put "work/lunch" or activity/lunch in one box.

e) **Sleep** = Be honest! Remember we want to see the true picture of a typical week.

f) **Home** = Input time you are at home. This can represent when you are spending time with family, friends, watching TV, cooking, bathing, chores, social media, reading, etc.

TIP: Table One "Pre-Work" (page 13): represents a normal schedule for you. If you are experiencing a different situation that would last for more than a month, then please put down that "new normal schedule". If you are experiencing a different situation that would last for less than a month, then put down your "regular normal" week. Use the categories listed on the example table ----

Work Activity Transit Lunch Sleep Home (page 13)

Use this space to write down key notes from what you just read.

Notes:

Fill in your table below:

TABLE ONE: PRE-WORK							
Time	Sun	Mon	Tues	Wed	Thurs	Fri	Sat
1am -6am							
7am							
8am							
9am							
10am							
11am							
12pm							
1pm							
2pm							
3pm							
4pm							
5pm							
6pm							
7pm							
8pm							
9pm							
10pm							
11pm							
12am							

Review my example tables: Goals and Pre-Work with filled in categorized items. I want you to review my typical week and hopefully it will help you with tracking your typical week. My **Activity** during the weekdays represents my daughter's karate class where there is a set time and date. My **Activity** for the weekend represents my set exercise time with set times and dates. The other days I exercise are based on my availability and I am not tied into a date and time frame.

Example Goals: Short Term, Mid and Long-Term

- I am a published author, so my writing my next book is always one of my goals
- Losing Weight and Learn about Nutrition
- Spend more family time with my girls

TABLE ONE "PRE-WORK": EXAMPLE							
Time	Sun	Mon	Tues	Wed	Thurs	Fri	Sat
1am – 6am	Sleep	Sleep	Sleep	Sleep	Sleep	Sleep	Sleep
7am	Sleep	Transit	Transit	Transit	Transit	Transit	Sleep
8am	Home	Work	Work	Work	Work	Work	Home
9am	Home	Work	Work	Work	Work	Work	Home
10am	Home	Work	Work	Work	Work	Work	Home
11am	Home	Work	Work	Work	Work	Work	Home
12noon	Transit	Work	Work	Work	Work	Work	Transit
1pm	Activity	Lunch	Lunch	Lunch	Lunch	Lunch	Activity
2pm	Activity	Work	Work	Work	Work	Work	Activity
3pm	Activity	Work	Work	Work	Work	Work	Activity
4pm	Activity	Work	Work	Work	Work	Work	Activity
5pm	Transit	Transit	Transit	Transit	Transit	Transit	Home
6pm	Home	Transit	Transit	Transit	Transit	Transit	Home
7pm	Home	Activity	Activity	Activity	Activity	Activity	Home
8pm	Home	Activity	Activity	Activity	Activity	Activity	Home
9pm	Home	Transit	Transit	Transit	Transit	Transit	Transit
10pm	Home	Home	Home	Home	Home	Home	Activity/ Transit
11pm	Sleep	Sleep	Sleep	Sleep	Sleep	Sleep	Sleep
12midnight	Sleep	Sleep	Sleep	Sleep	Sleep	Sleep	Sleep

Instructions for TABLE TWO: ANALYSIS OF PRE-WORK:

Table Two: We will now move into totaling your categorized items for each day. Do not change the gray shaded areas on the chart.

a) Each day represents a day's total of 24 hours. HINT: Input all your totals and subtract from 24 and this number will represent your **Sleep** hours.

b) Write down the total for each row. Add up all rows and they should total 168. Yes, we have 168 hours in one week.

Fill in your table below:

TABLE TWO:								
Items on schedule	Sun	Mon	Tues	Wed	Thurs	Fri	Sat	Hours
Activity								
Transit								
Lunch								
Work								
Sleep								
Home								
Total	24	24	24	24	24	24	24	168

Review my example table: Table Two

TABLE TWO: EXAMPLE								
Items on schedule	Sun	Mon	Tues	Wed	Thurs	Fri	Sat	Hours
Activity	4	2	2	2	2	2	4.5	18.5
Transit	2	4	4	4	4	4	2.5	24.5
Lunch	0	1	1	1	1	1	0	5
Work	0	8	8	8	8	8	0	40
Home	9	1	1	1	1	1	8	22
Sleep	9	8	8	8	8	8	9	58
Total	24	24	24	24	24	24	24	168

Use this space to write down key notes from what you just read.

Notes:

Now let's analyze your categorized items. Put the totals from "Table Two" into the "Analysis" table below.

Use a calculator with the following formula: Total from Table Two *divided by* Total Hours

Analysis	Total from Table Two	Total Hours		Total %
Activity		168		Reveals how you spend your time - look for opportunities for change or look at how you can accomplish every day task quicker and adding quality
Transit		168		
Lunch		168		
Work		168		
Sleep		168		
Home		168		

Results: Review percentage to rank your top and bottom; hint lunch should be your bottom every time

Warning signs
*sleep % (baseline = 33%)
*work % (baseline = 24%)
*lunch % (baseline = 3%)

Review my example table: Table Two to see my results.

Data Analysis EXAMPLE	Total from Table Two	Total from Table Two	Total %	
Activity	18.5	168	11%	
Transit	24.5	168	15%	Reveals how you spend your time - look for opportunities for change or look for how you can accomplish everyday tasks quicker and adding quality
Lunch	5	168	3%	
Work	40	168	24%	
Sleep	58	168	35%	
Home	22	168	13%	

Formula: Total from Table Two *divided by* Total from Table Two
Results: Review percentage to rank your top and bottom; hint lunch should be your bottom every time

Warning signs
*sleep % (baseline = 25% - 33%):
*To track your Sleep try to get a device that would determine how soundly you sleep vs restless sleep as well.
*work % (baseline = 24%)
*lunch % (baseline = 3%)

The results are in!

Let's use my example from the Data Analysis

Let's review the categories:

✓ **Activity** Percentage. This represents 11% of how time spent on activities.
TIP: Make sure this activity is valuable to your time and in alignment of your goals/dreams.

✓ **Transit** Percentage. This represents 15% of your week is spent in your car/transit.
TIP: If you unhappy about this percentage, begin to think about ways you can get this percentage down by adjusting your route for activities.

✓ **Home** Percentage. This represents 13% of your week is spent at home.
TIP: We will do a lot with this percentage in the next table. Have your short, mid and long-term goals (page 7) in your hand while we fill out the next table.

✓ **Lunch** Percentage. This represents 3% of your week is spent eating lunch.
TIP: We will do a lot with this percentage in the next table. Have your short, mid and long-term goals in your hand while we fill out the next table.

Let's review the categories:

✓ **Work** Percentage. This represents 24% of your week is spent outside of your home, making money. If you work from home, this should also represent those hours as well.
TIP: Make sure you are working towards your goals and financial goal so that this percentage is moving you towards them.

✓ **Sleep** Percentage. The chart above shows 35% for sleep which is a great percentage.
TIP: According to National Sleep Foundation – a person between the ages of 18 to 64 should get 6 – 11 hours a sleep every day.

Your results are in!

Write your Data Analysis below:

PHASE TWO:

(make sure you have TABLE ONE "Pre-Work" in front of you)

Now that we have analyzed your typical "normal week", let's get more involved with how time is spent while you are at Home. I chose the category titled Home, because this is the one area where you can be flexible with daily tasks and moments throughout the week. Also think about beginning to work towards a goal or introduce yourself to a new hobby.

Sunday	Monday	Tuesday	Wednesday	Thursday	Friday	Saturday

Notes: Did you think you had <u>this many hours</u> at home each day?

Instructions using the blank Table Three:

STEP ONE: Make sure you are viewing your Table One chart for this step. Count the number of times you are **Home**, which will tell you right away how much free/flexible time you have in your normal week. I know this may be surprising especially if you did think you had no extra time or maybe you felt like your days all blended together. Phase Two will introduce you to the "new you". It will give you the opportunity to fill in activities you want to incorporate into your week. Remember your **Goals: Short Term, Mid and Long-Term as well**

See the example below: I am using my Example Table One Chart to fill in the number of times I am at **Home.**

Sun	Mon	Tues	Wed	Thurs	Fri	Sat	Total hours
9	1	1	1	1	1	8	
# of times Home is listed	# of times Home is listed	# of times Home is listed	# of times Home is listed	# of times Home is listed	# of times Home is listed	# of times Home is listed	22

TABLE ONE: EXAMPLE							
Time	Sun	Mon	Tues	Wed	Thurs	Fri	Sat
1am	Sleep	Sleep	Sleep	Sleep	Sleep	Sleep	Sleep
2am	Sleep	Sleep	Sleep	Sleep	Sleep	Sleep	Sleep
3am	Sleep	Sleep	Sleep	Sleep	Sleep	Sleep	Sleep
4am	Sleep	Sleep	Sleep	Sleep	Sleep	Sleep	Sleep
5am	Sleep	Sleep	Sleep	Sleep	Sleep	Sleep	Sleep
6am	Sleep	Sleep	Sleep	Sleep	Sleep	Sleep	Sleep
7am	Sleep	Transit	Transit	Transit	Transit	Transit	Sleep
8am	Home	Work	Work	Work	Work	Work	Home
9am	Home	Work	Work	Work	Work	Work	Home
10am	Home	Work	Work	Work	Work	Work	Home
11am	Home	Work	Work	Work	Work	Work	Home
12noon	Transit	Work	Work	Work	Work	Work	Transit
1pm	Activity	Lunch	Lunch	Lunch	Lunch	Lunch	Activity
2pm	Activity	Work	Work	Work	Work	Work	Activity
3pm	Activity	Work	Work	Work	Work	Work	Activity
4pm	Activity	Work	Work	Work	Work	Work	Activity
5pm	Transit	Transit	Transit	Transit	Transit	Transit	Home
6pm	Home	Transit	Transit	Transit	Transit	Transit	Home
7pm	Home	Activity	Activity	Activity	Activity	Activity	Home
8pm	Home	Activity	Activity	Activity	Activity	Activity	Home
9pm	Home	Transit	Transit	Transit	Transit	Transit	Transit
10pm	Home	Home	Home	Home	Home	Home	Activity/ Transit
11pm	Sleep	Sleep	Sleep	Sleep	Sleep	Sleep	Sleep
12midnight	Sleep	Sleep	Sleep	Sleep	Sleep	Sleep	Sleep

STEP TWO: This step will allow you to fill in the activities you can do at **Home** or think about new things you would add to your week. Notice that Table Three does not go by TIME but it shows HOURS. Showing hours gives flexibility to do these activities. Now you can take a look at your short, mid and long-term goals and dreams, including your financial goals to fill out Table Three.

TABLE THREE: *Count the # of Home boxes from table one*							
Hours	Sun	Mon	Tues	Wed	Thurs	Fri	Sat
1							
2							
3							
4							
5							
6							
7							
8							
9							
10							
11							
12							
13							
14							
15							

Review the Example Table Three before you fill in your chart.

Look at the example table below: I have listed all my **Sunday activities; the rest of the table is blocked with a black highlighted cell**. I am making sure that these activities are in direct alignment with my goals. TIP: Keep in mind that you can leave the house to go to these new or existing flexible activities.

Example Goals: Short Term, Mid and Long-Term

- I am a published author, so my writing my next book is always one of my goals
- Losing Weight and Learn about Nutrition
- Spend more family time with my girls

My observations:

3 hours of family time - 1 hour of writing - one hour of reading - one hour for organizing the week – one hour for networking - one hour for napping and one hour for exercise

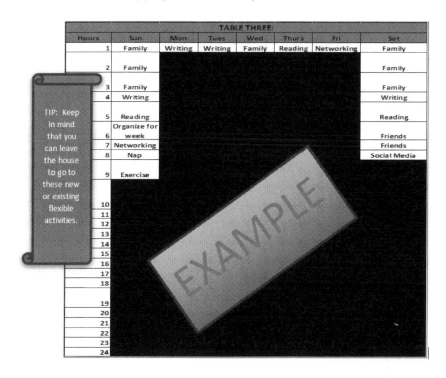

TABLE THREE:

Hours	Sun	Mon	Tues	Wed	Thurs	Fri	Sat
1	Family	Writing	Writing	Family	Reading	Networking	Family
2	Family						Family
3	Family						Family
4	Writing						Writing
5	Reading						Reading
6	Organize for week						Friends
7	Networking						Friends
8	Nap						Social Media
9	Exercise						
10							
11							
12							
13							
14							
15							
16							
17							
18							
19							
20							
21							
22							
23							
24							

TIP: Keep in mind that you can leave the house to go to these new or existing flexible activities.

EXAMPLE

PHASE THREE: *(Make sure you refer to your TABLE THREE)*

Instructions using the blank Table Four:

STEP ONE: Make sure you are viewing your Table Three chart for this step. List each activity in the first column and then count how many times you do the activity each day. Phase Three will give you more insight if you are on your way of achieving your goals/dreams.

From my Table one – I had 22 hours at **Home.**

Review my example table four below:

Activities	Sun	Mon	Tues	Wed	Thurs	Fri	Sat	Hours
TABLE FOUR: EXAMPLE								
FAMILY	3			1			3	7
WRITING	1	1	1				1	4
READING	1				1		1	3
ORGANIZE FOR WEEK	1							1
NETWORKING	1					1		2
NAP	1							1
SOCIAL MEDIA							1	1
EXERCISE	1							1
FRIENDS							2	2
Total	9	1	1	1	1	1	8	22 matches Home
From Table Two (minus home/sleep)	6	15	15	15	15	15	7	88
From Table Two Sleep	9	8	8	8	8	8	9	58
Total Day	24	24	24	24	24	24	24	168

Review my example table four analysis below:

Data Analysis EXAMPLE – TABLE FOUR					
ACTIVITIES	HOURS FROM TABLE FOUR	DIVIDED BY	TOTAL HOURS AT HOME	Total %	Reveals how you spend your time - look for opportunities for change or look for how you can accomplish everyday task quicker and adding quality
FAMILY	7	/	22	32%	
WRITING	4	/	22	18%	
READING	3	/	22	14%	
ORGANIZE FOR WEEK	1	/	22	5%	
NETWORKING	2	/	22	9%	
NAP	1	/	22	5%	
SOCIAL MEDIA	1	/	22	5%	
EXERCISE	1	/	22	5%	
FRIENDS	2	/	22	9%	

Results: Review percentage to rank your top and bottom; hint lunch should be your bottom every time (smile)

Review Activity, Transit and Home and plan to discuss percentages at session.

The results are in! Let's use my example from the Data Analysis Table Four below.

<u>Let's review my goals and dreams:</u>

During this time in my life, I working on my third book and also knew that I had to stay focus on being with my family and not sacrifice time away from them but intentionally spending time with them while I achieved one of my personal life goals and dreams.

- ✓ Family is #1 for me!
- ✓ Book publication is #2! You will see that Reading comes in a close third. Research and my experience show that writing and reading goes hand in hand. I like to read all topics to strengthen my own writing abilities.
- ✓ Networking & Friends are tied which makes sense since I am usually networking with my friends and meeting new people to include in my circle. It is extremely important as an entrepreneur to establish relationships and partnerships with others.
- ✓ All other activities are tied at 5%.

Keep in mind that these activities can be changed and should align with your goals and dreams.

Fill in your table four below:

Data Analysis – TABLE FOUR					
ACTIVITIES	HOURS FROM TABLE FOUR	DIVIDED BY	TOTAL HOURS AT HOME	TOTAL %	
		/			
		/			
		/			Reveals how you spend your time - look for opportunities for change or look for how you can accomplish everyday task quicker and adding quality
		/			
		/			
		/			
		/			
		/			
		/			
		/			
		/			
		/			
		/			
		/			
		/			
Results: Review percentage to rank your top and bottom; hint lunch should be your bottom every time (smile) Review Activity, Transit and Home and plan to discuss percentages at session.					

Review your activities,

Do they line up with your

Goals and Dreams?

Your results are in! Write your results Data Analysis Table Four:

List your results from Table Four

Let's now review our Objectives to make sure we have accomplished our learning.

---

3 Highlights:

✓ Review your short, mid and long-term goals that you will achieve. The time you tracked should show how you are accomplishing these goals. Remember, if you find a disconnect as you fill in your weekly table and your goals, then you should re-think what you do every week that do not align with your goals. Also include a financial goal as well.

✓ Do you see your dreams coming true using your tables? Dare to dream and see how can find time to achieve these dreams.

✓ Review your intentional and memorable moments in your life. Begin to embrace your authentic friendships and relationships where you will be present in the moments and not feel overwhelmed or double booked.

Congratulations on completing the steps in becoming a Manager of Your Time! I hope you enjoyed journey with me. Are you motivated to achieve your goals and dreams?

Let's answer the questions that were asked at the beginning of this journey. Do you have free time to be adventurous? What if someone calls you with an emergency, can you truly be there for that person?

 Put down your detailed answers to the questions above:

The New You:

- o Remember to fulfill your short, mid and long-term goals that you want to achieve. Including your financial goal as well. Achieve your goals and manager your time properly.
- o You have made room for your dreams. Continue to dare to dream and see how you can find time to achieve these dreams.
- o Begin to create intentional and memorable moments in your life that will give you authentic friendships and relationships where you will be present in the moments and not feel overwhelmed or double booked.

Many people say that "Time got away from me?"

What are some of your responses when someone asks you about your time?

*Create intentional
memories every day*

****

ABOUT THE AUTHOR

MS. BENITA SMITH

- Email: CoachBenitaS@gmail.com
- Instagram: @CoachBenitaS
- Life Coach specializing in transforming Communication between Mothers & Daughters

Time Management is a personal subject for me. It is essential that I share this simple and easy process with you, so that you can live your life now. Many people feel they must wait for a milestone to begin to live. Have you heard "When I retire, I will start to travel the world"? If you are reading this right now, you can begin to live today. My purpose is to make sure you are creating great memories for those around you because memories last forever.

Made in the USA
Columbia, SC
22 May 2020

98152707R00026